T0274810

ANOTHER LAST CALL
poems on addiction & deliverance

edited by
Kaveh Akbar
& Paige Lewis

SARABANDE BOOKS ⬤ LOUISVILLE, KENTUCKY

Publisher's Cataloging-In-Publication Data
(Provided by Cassidy Cataloguing Services, Inc.).

Names: Akbar, Kaveh, editor. | Lewis, Paige, editor.
Title: Another last call : poems on addiction & deliverance / edited by Kaveh Akbar & Paige Lewis.
Description: First edition. | Louisville, Kentucky : Sarabande Books, [2023]
Identifiers: ISBN: 978-1-956046-16-8 (paperback) | 978-1-956046-17-5 (ebook)
Subjects: LCSH: Alcoholism--Poetry. | Substance abuse--Poetry. | Addicts--Family relationships-- Poetry. | Alcoholism--Treatment--Poetry. | Substance abuse--Treatment--Poetry. | LCGFT: Poetry.
Classification: LCC: PS595.A24 A56 2023 | DDC: 811.008/0355--dc23

Cover and interior design by Danika Isdahl.
Printed in USA.
This book is printed on acid-free paper.
Sarabande Books is a nonprofit literary organization.

Acknowledgments in order of appearance:

"Running" from An American Sunrise. Originally in The New Yorker (July 9, 2018). Copyright © 2018, 2019 by Joy Harjo. Used by permission of W. W. Norton & Company, Inc.

"This Shit Is Not Interesting" and "Requiem for Guy" by Bernardo Wade copyright © 2023 by Bernardo Wade. Reprinted with the permission of the author.

"A Recovery Guide for Adult Children of Alcoholics" by Megan Denton Ray copyright © 2020 by Megan Denton Ray. First ublished in Muzzle Magazine. Reprinted with the permission of the author.

"Trouble House" by Megan Denton Ray copyright © 2017 by Megan Denton Ray. First published in Salt Hill Journal. Reprinted with permission of the author.

"i" and "ii." by Jos Charles. Copyright © 2023. Reprinted with the permission of the author.

"Dominion" by Afaa M. Weaver copyright © 2023 by Afaa M. Weaver. Reprinted with permission of the author.

"On Alcohol" from Madness by sam sax, copyright © 2017 by sam sax. Used by permission of Penguin Books, an imprint of Penguin Publishing Group, a division of Penguin Random House LLC. All rights reserved.

"Palinode" by sam sax copyright © 2023 by sam sax. Reprinted with permission of the author.

"The Walnut House" by Marianne Chan copyright © 2023 by Marianne Chan. First published in Kenyon Review. Forthcoming in Leaving Biddle City (Sarabande Books, 2024). Reprinted with permission of the author.

"The Cannon on the Hood of My Father's Car", from Floaters: Poems by Martín Espada. copyright © 2021 by Martín Espada. Used by permission of W. W. Norton & Company, Inc.

"The Bouncer's Confession" by Martín Espada copyright © 1996 by Martín Espada.Reprinted with the permission of the author.

TABLE OF CONTENTS

INTRODUCTION

When asked about the difficulties of sculpture, Michelangelo said it was easy, he just chipped away everything that wasn't David.

If you erase in reverse, you're revealing. Both erasing and revealing are ways of showing what always existed. Erasing says, "I shall chisel away the marble to free the *David*." Revelation says, "You are the chisel."

It's easy to cut things out of a life. Relatively. You break up with a shitty partner, quit eating bread, delete the Twitter app. You cut it out, and the shape of what's really killing you clarifies a little. The whole Abrahamic world invests itself in this promise: don't lie, don't cheat or steal or kill, and you'll be a good person. Eight of the ten commandments are about what thou shalt not. But you can live a whole life not doing any of that stuff and still avoid doing any good. That's the whole crisis, the misguided belief that goodness is built on a kind of constructed absence, not-doing. That belief corrupts everything, has everyone with any power sitting on their hands. A rich man goes a whole day without directly violently striking an unhoused person with his own hands and so goes to sleep content in his goodness. In another world, he's buying crates of socks and Clif Bars and tents, distributing them in city centers. But for him, abstinence reigns.

Normal people think of recovery as a kind of abstinence: they imagine us in recovery sitting around white-knuckled, sweating as we count our hours trying desperately to distract ourselves enough to not relapse. This is because for normal people, drinking is an activity, like slicing an onion or watching TV. They can reasonably imagine excising drinking, like any other activity, without collapsing their entire person.

For a drunk, there's nothing but drink. For an addict, there's nothing but the drug. For me (Kaveh), there was nothing in my life that wasn't predicated on getting drunk—either getting fucked up itself or getting money to get fucked up by working or slinging this drug for that drug or that drug for cash. There was nothing of my life that wasn't set in motion by that narcotic gravity.

Getting sober means having to figure out how to spend twenty-four hours a day. It means building an entirely new personality, learning how to move your face, your fingers. It means learning how to eat, how to speak among people and walk and love and more than any of that, learning how to just sit still. You're moving into a house the last tenants trashed. You spend all your time ripping up the piss-carpet, filling in the holes in the wall, *and* you also somehow have to remember to feed yourself and make rent and not kick every person who talks to you in the face. There's no abstinence in it. There's no self-will. It's a chisel. It's surrender to the chisel. Of course you don't hope to come out a David. It's miracle enough to emerge still standing on two feet.

For many of the poets assembled here, poetry was a place to put themselves while on that journey. Joy Priest writes, "I'm 31 days sober, deciding to lead myself / beyond January." Sophie Klahr writes, "I am a waiting room, crowded with sound." Language is a place to go as the new self forms, a safe place to store a body and mind.

My brain—the same organ that controls my breathing and my heartbeat and the contractions of my intestinal muscles—*that's* the organ that wants me to drink and use again. What hope does language have against such a formidable foe? What hope is there in self-will, in abstinence?

The only hope I've found is in other people. Nobody gets sober in a vacuum, and that's why when Sarabande approached us about doing this anthology, it felt important to everyone that I, an addict in sober recovery for nearly a decade, work alongside my spouse and partner, Paige Lewis, whose life has been inflected by my addiction and recovery nearly as much as my own. That's the thing about addiction—the addict is only one of a wide web of people whose lives are indelibly changed by their disease.

For countless poets in this anthology, it's not their own experience of addiction that's altered the trajectory of their living, but the suffering of a beloved. Poet Airea D. Matthews writes of "large lots of unbeing- / passed // down one generation to / the next." Steven Espada Dawson opens a poem called "My Brother Stole Every Spoon in the House" by saying, "so we don't eat soup anymore." The shadow of addiction is almost always larger than the life of the addict, and many of the voices gathered here testify to loving a person from that lightless, desperate place.

This anthology is by no means an exhaustive volume or even a representative one. What it feels like to us is a poetry mixtape, lovingly curated and organized for you, dear reader, that it might usefully illuminate or complicate or accompany you in your living. Reading, making yourself permeable to these poets' voices—that is decidedly active, and opposite the relative passivity of abstinence. Addicts are not bad people struggling to get good, they're sick people struggling to get well. As Diane Seuss writes in one of her poems contained here: "Where's the melody / to remedy the melody, the remedy to remedy the remedy?"

Here are sixty poems, some written by people actively battling addiction, some written by people who've been sober for years or decades, and others still written by poets who do not identify as addicts themselves but love or have loved addicted persons. Each poem in this volume fits in one of these three categories; that is the only organizing conceit Paige and I had in its curation. Besides that, we make no claims at objectivity—these are poems, written in English by still-living poets (remove either of those modifiers and the size of the book balloons) that both of us love. Organizing them has been a wellspring of experience, strength, and hope for us, giving us myriad occasions for meditation and contemplation and laughter and reflection. It is our fervent hope, in putting the anthology into the world now, that you too may find yourself accompanied by these voices.

—Kaveh Akbar & Paige Lewis

SAMHSA's National Helpline, 1-800-662-HELP (4357) (also known as the Treatment Referral Routing Service), or TTY: 1-800-487-4889, is a confidential, free, 24-hour-a-day, 365-day-a-year information service, in English and Spanish, for individuals and family members facing mental and/or substance use disorders. This service provides referrals to local treatment facilities, support groups, and community-based organizations.

Joy Harjo

Running

It's closing time. Violence is my boyfriend
With a cross to bear
        Hoisted on by the church.
He wears it everywhere.
There are no female deities in the Trinity.
      I don't know how I'm going to get out of here,
Said the flying fish to the tree.
          Last call.
We've had it with history, we who look for vision here
In the Indian and poetry bar, somewhere
To the left of Hell.
Now I have to find my way, when there's a river to cross and no
Boat to get me there, when there appears to be no home at all.
          My father gone, chased
By the stepfather's gun. *Get out of here.*
I've found my father at the bar, his ghost at least, some piece
Of him in this sorry place. The boyfriend's convincing to a crowd.
Right now, he's the spell of attraction. What tales he tells.
In the fog of thin hope, I wander this sad world
We've made with the enemy's words.
The lights quiver,
          Like they do when the power's dwindling to a
    dangling string.
It is time to go home. We are herded like stoned cattle, like
    children for the bombing drill—
        Out the door, into the dark street of this old Indian town
Where there are no Indians anymore.
I was afraid of the dark, because then I could see
        Everything. The truth with its eyes staring

Back at me. The mouth of the dark with its shiny moon teeth,
No words, just a hiss and a snap.
I could hear my heart hurting
With my *in-the-dark ears.*
I thought I could take it. Where was the party?
It's been a century since we left home with the American soldiers at
our backs.
The party had long started up in the parking lot.
He flew through the dark, broke my stride with a punch.
I went down then came up.
I thought I could take being a girl with her heart in her
Arms. I carried it for justice. For the rights of all Indians.
We all had that cross to bear.
Those Old Ones followed me, the quiet girl with the long dark hair,
The daughter of a warrior who wouldn't give up.
I wasn't ready yet, to fling free the cross

I ran and I ran through the 2 a.m. streets.

It was my way of breaking free. I was anything but history.
I was the wind.

This Shit Is Not Interesting

Sometimes when it's this dark,
         I light matches & let them
burn the tips of my fingers
         while I watch the flame—

this is what I know about memory.
         It flickers when it feels
like it. I've tried to forget that bare-
         knuckle night I left work,

thanking Nick for the quality
         of his daiquiris. He had
a toothy smile—he's gone now,
         a story for another night.

Though I should've stayed
         for another drink, I went
to meet Slim before the achy chills
         started from my neck

down to the soles of my feet.
         Here, I'd like to remind you
of the time Richard Pryor lights
         a match, you know, at the end

of *Live on the Sunset Strip*,
         he says, *What is that? Richard Pryor*
running down the street, & just like
         that we're taught to admire

another man's defeat. People will ask
          their boogeyman to step
into the light, laugh at the first stone
          thrown—paying for a seat.

This shit is not interesting
          to the ones who know, offstage
Pryor danced on the teeth
          of his deceits, slipping into spells

of regret. & I, who'd disappeared
          that week, got her text & flew
across town because I knew
          this time she was serious:

she'd thrown my shit behind
          the dumpster—a place I won't
soon forget—hold on, let's say a prayer
          for the brothers who don't

make it. God, bless those whose
          hot blood tests the blue lights
knifing through the night.
          Amen to these men, who bare

teeth at life. Thus, when I turned down
          the one-way on Dorgenois Street,
the same street nine years later
          I mourned a beloved killed by

a drunk driver, a driver who could
          have been me, I saw those cops
& I thought *run* but then thought
          gun. So instead, I pulled over,

thinking, *I'm in for it all right.* Knew it
        was my turn to boogeyman
into the light, so I lifted my hands up
        just right, fingers spread so wide

you might have thought I was aflame.
        I imagine the match Pryor lights
for the crowd, its sulfur smelled
        like *good night.* When I heard 12

close the car door, I felt the weight
        of Slim's package—
enough for a bid—wedged
        in my waistband, hidden,

unlike the belongings I'd never see
        again. Then he said, *Move & you're done.*
Before I blinked, the click
        of cuffs snapped against

my wrists. He pulled my shirt just so,
        & I felt the waistband
flick. *Fuck* fell from my lips
        as I watched the little bag of powder

drift between me & the 12 with fire.
        When he smiled, I heard a round
of applause. Pryor holds the match,
        & I swear, I see him flinch. I wasn't

surprised when I saw Resisting Arrest
        on those multicolored sheets.
Ain't but a few hours of peacocking
        before I felt that familiar ache—

cold sweats, jonesin', a yearn
           for death filled my stomach
as I crouched down near a man,
           who after thirty minutes of complaining

about his baby momma's expired tags
           noticed the animal writhing.
I lie so childlike, I can almost taste
           my mother's gumbo on Christmas Day,

& how a soft blanket might feel
           against my skin. I know, I know
this shit is not interesting
           unless you know the warmth

that comes when a stranger
           takes his coat & covers your body
on a jailhouse floor.

Requiem for Guy

After Katrina, we broke
into a FEMA trailer, a haven
filled with burn holes scattered
like little graves. I watched you
wrestle the TV antenna, smiling
because, for at least a few hours,
we summoned the soft hum
that sweet-talks bravado off
the brow, sedating our baby-faced
resentments with one another.
What did we know of friendship
but its malice? Once a week
we robbed the first to fall asleep,
reprieved, inevitably, by the need
to forgive the other's suffering.
This kind of love persists,
watching a man drift from life
into its seam, choking down breath,
maybe in a dream where junkies dance
on a blank slate. We were joyful
when you'd get a call, hopping in
your girlfriend's car to go somewhere
else & smoke cigarettes till
we had more small pills staring
back from our palms. Today,
one of my students told me,
You're my guy, but I thought of you
& how many sticky afternoons
we tried to forget our names, handing

them back to God so we could
rest. When I got the call, I knew
He had refused to give yours back.

Megan Denton Ray

A Recovery Guide for Adult Children of Alcoholics

Dream your father relapses
and checks himself into a facility
because he can't take care of you and Emily
anymore. Dream your mother comes to pick you up
and suddenly you're in her Mark III conversion van,
pine green, swerving down a narrow
canyon road and the van has almost fallen off
the edge—over and over and over—but somehow
bounces back to the middle of the road, cartoonlike—over
and over and over. And you and Emily are crying
and Mom says everything is okay
but you realize that she is also drunk
and she is laughing and there is no safe place to go
and she keeps drinking mouthwash
from tiny plastic cups with tiny plastic lids
and promises it's not vodka. It's Listerine.
        Dear one,
remember that all fear feels the same: right before
you get hit by a car, or when someone leaves you, and—
I'd imagine—right before you die. Remember to swirl
around it in a clockwise direction with a lamp
in your throat. Remember that radiance will fall
on us all with the strength and delicacy
of lace. With heat lightning. With blue lights flashing
and your mother slumped over the steering wheel.
        Your father slumped over the steering wheel
in the dream where he blacked out for three hours—no, the
not-dream—where he blacked out for three hours and drove
through town, then hit the neighbor's brick mailbox

so close to home. He was so close to home. The policeman
tapping at his window. Your father
in the back of a cop car and off to jail he goes.
       Dear one,
try holding on to the fire this time. Try pulling raindrops
back into the earth. Try thanking the neighbor
for not pressing charges. For keeping the secret.
For checking in on the children from time to time.
       Dear one,
are you still there?—Those with pennies
who look for pennies? The god who hears me
when I cough? There is a reason for good juice
and toast. For putting flowers all over the house.
Must I ration my wellness?

Trouble House

I was nine when the angels visited. My mother was there,
sleeping with the TV on, in the bed from Havertys—

the one with the tall posts carved like pineapples.
My father was there beside her, brooding—lonely

as a severed thumb. My mother was recovering. No,
relapsing. She was panting underwater, fumbling

her bone barrettes. My father only wanted a bed made
of cherrywood. And he never forgave me for the time

I swung, wildly in my pajamas, around one of the posts
until I heard it snap. That was the night the angels visited.

Suddenly, a light through my bedroom window, there
at the Trouble House—not a street light or the moon.

It was wide and warm, a great white *whoosh* of a thing.
I felt my cheeks go pink, red ribbons around my wrists.

I saw myself as a shining lady, all emeralds and pulp.
I saw my mother crying after my father pawned

her ruby rings. I saw all *my* treasures: rose quartz, bees,
broken glass. I used to carry them in a Crown Royal bag.

We were a Crown Royal family—rich in purple and gold.
And God was there. He was. He parked his great sedan

right in front of the Trouble House. He beeped his horn, and I came running wildly, in my pajamas.

i.

I passed, in my way, a night or two, make-shift, cowed in rain.

I put everything, I tried, into the book.

Occasionally, a frock I etched prayer upon: I preferred the few sweetnesses there.

I saw the exits, I heard the bell, and dug deeper still.

And I loved it.

I learned nothing is holier than nothing.

To flinch at the wind, observe.

ii.

Looking back through the between of leaves, quantity sits silent before capacity.

Ashuwet brushes the arm.

The nativity in the yard has no baby in it.

Runs to the shore, no self-medicating anymore.

Appointments at the clinic, no longer on the side of kings.

Boys form triangles in parking lots whilst this thing—dark water, dark age—closes o'er our head.

We are on the side of ghosts of kings.

Afaa M. Weaver

Dominion

In between the leaves of a weeping willow tree,
a rock from outer space sets its sights on me,
rattling like a crazed bumble bee on crack,
hardened on broken backs, it sets out to smack
me down. The long rip and tear it makes along
the space where my nose falls off, like a thong
between two unruly cheeks, it rips until the sweet
vapor of a gangsta nirvana comes again to meet
the devil riding high on the rim of the hole in me.

On Alcohol

my first drink was in my mother
my next, my bris. doctor spread red
wine across my lips. took my foreskin

      ::

every time i drink   i lose something

      ::

no one knows the origins of alcohol. tho surely an accident
before sacrament. agricultural apocrypha. enough grain stored up
for it to get weird in the cistern. rot gospel. god water.

      ::

brandy was used to treat everything
from colds to pneumonia
frostbite to snake bites

tb patients were placed on ethanol drips
tonics & cough medicines
spooned into the crying mouths of children

      ::

each friday in synagogue a prayer for red
at dinner, the cemetery, the kitchen
spirits

      ::

how many times have i woke
strange in an unfamiliar bed?
my head neolithic

::

my grandfather died with a bottle in one hand
& flowers in the other. he called his drink his medicine
he called his woman
                    she locked the door

::

i can only half blame alcohol for my overdose
the other half is my own hand
that poured the codeine   that lifted the red plastic again & again &

::

i'm trying to understand pleasure   it comes back
in flashes   every jean button thumbed open to reveal
a different man   every slurred & furious permission

::

i was sober a year before [   ] died

::

every time i drink   i lose someone

::

23

if you look close at the process of fermentation
you'll see tiny animals destroying the living body
until it's transformed into something more volatile

                    ::

the wino outside the liquor store
mistakes me for his son

Palinode

it's not i don't not have a problem
nor is it my problem isn't not me
neither is there anything in the meat
that denies us all this theater
but here in the keloid i remember
what pride i took in those four years
i believed in control & in substance
then i was a lady out amidst teething
in the bars' crooked dentistry
i'd sip still water & become greater
than any man pulling fishes from stone
there beside the other dying
parishioners i was perfected, sober
as a judge in his grave haunting
the bars like a spirit as evenings
dragged open their pupils in the dark
i'd let any man talk dirty but none
take me home knowing we'd wake
different in the same bed, who am i
now i've returned to the well, unwell.
how sad & predictable it was a man
who brought me? after four years
i let him offer an exit wound
& climbed greedy through the soft tissue
grateful to have again found someone
else to blame— —for a time addict
was my name, it fit like an orange life
jacket, now it is gone i am gone—
& who the hell is this new self
that's come to fill my absence?

The Walnut House

We wanted our own place. So, we lived on Walnut Street and took theater classes at the community college. Sam was a good actor, could bring life to Shakespeare, make his meanings clear. We drank walnut wine on Walnut Street

and invited people over. The house was owned by Homer, but this is no epic. This is a flat, nonnarrative, Midwestern conversation, the likes of which we had every day that year, the long winding talks a person could enter with little effort, a path in a field

with no hill or knotty roots. But I could make this an epic. I could build into it a journey plot, if necessary. It was 2007. We were nineteen and twenty, and we ruined Homer's house with our boredom.

Homer never came by to pick up rent. Why was that? He was seventy and did push-ups on our back porch. He'd renovated the house before we moved in. He'd done all that work. And we drank too much and flushed tampons

down the toilet, our friends vomiting on the kitchen tile. By 2008, the walls in the Walnut house were stained and crumbling like rotting teeth. What is the opposite of an epic? A lyric? Lyric poetry is not the opposite, but just another type, another option.

Some would say we could've chosen another type of coming-of-age story. We didn't need the underage lotus-eaters drinking wine on our porch, breaking the staircase banister. Didn't need the afternoons spent nursing the headache, bike stolen, the smell

of smoke and Michigan leaves, the color of cheddar cheese,
plummeting down our driveway. Perhaps Sam and I could've
moved to Chicago. We could've auditioned for plays at the
Steppenwolf. Sam was truly a good actor, could cry

on command. But perhaps it could've been worse on Walnut
Street. We could've died from raw chicken on the counter,
someone could've broken a hip from all the dancing, someone
could've drunk from the wrong cup, and yet, we made it out alive.

Martín Espada

The Cannon on the Hood of My Father's Car

The football coach taught Driver's Ed. He would hear a siren pass and say:
There goes another one. He meant me. I mowed down the rubber cones
as if they marched at me, an orange army invading from an orange planet.
My head snapped with every curb I hit, a speed bag for the fist I never saw.

I failed Driver's Ed, *F* like father, *F* like Frank, my father's name. My father
now would have to teach me how to drive. He said: *I'd like to mount a cannon*
on the hood of my car, swivel it around, and blast all the bad drivers off the road.
He meant me. So I learned to drive, one eye on the quaking of his chin, the cords
in his neck, waiting for him to shred my learner's permit so it fluttered in my face.

A taxi dropped him off one morning. *You have to drive me back to the city,*
he said. *I lost my car.* At the age of five or so, I lost my turtle under the bed.
My father found the creature, crawling on his fingertips, still trying to escape.
JFK was president in 1962, but my father was the finder of lost turtles.

I tucked my learner's permit in my shirt pocket and drove him to the city.
I read the stubble on his chin. My father, who silenced the room whenever he
spoke, said nothing, years before the AA meeting where he stood up and said:
Hello, my name is Frank. We drove around the same block three times before
I said: *There it is.* Someone tore the cannon off the hood. That's why we missed it.

The Bouncer's Confession

I know about the Westerns
where stunt doubles belly flop
through banisters rigged to collapse
or crash through chairs designed to splinter.
A few times the job was like that.
A bone fragment still floats
in my right ring finger
because the human skull
is harder than any fist.

Mostly, I stood watch at the door
and imagined their skulls
brimming with alcohol
like divers drowning in their own helmets.
Their heads would sag, shaking
to stay awake, elbows sliding out
across the bar.
I gathered their coats. I found their hats.
I rolled up their paper bags
full of sacred objects only I could see.
I interrogated them for an address,
a hometown. I called the cab,
I slung an arm across my shoulders
to walk them down the stairs.

One face still wakes me some mornings.
I remember black-frame eyeglasses
off-balance, his unwashed hair.
I remember the palsy that made claws

of his hands, that twisted his mouth
in the trembling parody of a kiss.

I remember the stack of books he read
beside the beer he would not stop drinking.
I remember his fainted face
pressed against the bar.
This time, I dragged a corkscrewed body
slowly down the stairs, hugged to my ribs,
his books in my other hand,
only to see the impatient taxi
pulling away. I yelled at acceleration smoke,
then fumbled the body with the books
back up the stairs, and called the cab again.

No movie barrooms. No tall stranger
shot the body spread-eagled across the broken table.
No hero, with a hero's uppercut, knocked them out,
not even me. I carried them out.

Branches

And suddenly, expectedly, mothers started
to reach their arms—fists to elbows—down
their children's mouths and throats and into
the sugar-laden lining of the stomach.
Fathers did too;

                  husbands their wives'
their husbands' throats; sisters their brothers'
their mothers'; and my brothers even reached
into a man on the street with a paper crane.
We'd been told we would find some new

                          pleasure
there. We had a notion the insides held answers
to all our untenable questions. A teenager might
go missing for days. Her mother would plunge
down the tongues

                of the kid's friends; the missing
girl's sister alone in a bedroom would choke
on her own crackling elbows as she grasped
for what she'd forgotten.

                  Each time an arm
was pulled out of a mouth, it came coated:
In short, the limb once inside made a cast
like a silicone mold

                of whatever it touched:
Impressions like pink dish-washing gloves
made of blood guts and dinner

                      drew out
of the head like a yawn: The coating sloughed
whole off the arm: It peeled off intact as a swim
cap, thick as wax and wriggling

                            with rubbery veins.
People would squeeze off these casts and leave
them indiscriminately anywhere.
                            They called
these the branch of an arm for their likenesses
to roots, to the trunks of young trees. Streets
were littered with branches.
                         In living rooms
people made shelves of the things. Having
been asked through the stomach
                         for answers
I myself grew a crop of unreachable questions.
I phoned Mother, told her I'd be coming home
soon,
then got ahold of her spleen and found
nothing. I left her with those first little branches
dripping, inspected, and thrown on the eaves.
I branched out to others: my sister
                         whose roof
in Houston thatched casts of her and her husband's
and her little boys' innards;
                       sequences of strangers
whose bare-naked knees ground my rug to its stitches
who entered through any obtainable hole
                         dropped
into me for answers and left empty-handed
the veins on their fingers in the cracks of my grin.
I reached out to the preacher but found only wafers
and prison-grade beef.
                     I littered the drippings
of politicians and recycled a stack of historians'
suppers.

Of late I've been thinking around
the question of my sensitive lover's insides.
I haven't reached often

            though I wouldn't say
never (his fifth and sixth kidneys are swinging
on cords over the sink to dry; I reached deep)
but not lately or again:

            We could make us a pact
to prevent reaching: could stitch half our fingers
together: could start fresh from *So nice to meet you.*
See my lips—how they part like a seed. Listen
as I ask him to balance his fingers on the buds
at the tip of my tongue.

            Watch how I trust the gap
in his teeth without seeing whether my fist
might fit through them. We could stop

                at the space
at the edge of a lip with the trace of our fathers
stitched into our hides: intestines in circles
that coil round our feet: with the sleeves
of their innards

            as punctuation for our pores
their hair in the thick of our skin we could listen.

Every Song You'd Play While High Is Haunted Now

Shit, the blinds open, the rags wet with soot,
or your robot vacuum sucking circles in carpet.
Baby's got a playlist running in the background
so suddenly
           this day of dusting into the spring
smells less like Lysol and more like a dollar bill
rolled tight, rimmed with a week's worth of snot,
a pinch of blood.
           You don't know in the moment
why your busy lover rolling his PJs to the knees
seems the image of a wake, as if his funny wink
when he looks up at you were imagined: a face
in a casket staring. My God
           is the minor key made
of actual demons? It goes A, B♭, comedown sharp.
It comprises a short list of songs that could kill,
and every time one plays, its key signature thumps
in your veins like phone-lit nights in high school
spent playing Russian roulette
           with a bag of blow.
You plucked at that white hill to spite your pulse.
You figured your first love would die of an OD,
held him anyway, and were right.
           Your second man
would never think of you *like that*, so you slapped
a bag rocky with powder against your thigh, secured
it with Scotch tape, and took a plane anywhere,
though you'd be back.
           Addiction is an urge for noise

that sounds ended when it begins. Which makes it
harder, when baby plays certain songs, to stay clean
and sober in dry daylight:

                     the water-stained windows
open out into winter's last breeze. It may be spring,
so this house will be clean by the inch, but what lasts.

Joshua Mehigan

Cold Turkey

They're over now forever, the long dances.
Our woods are quiet. The god is gone tonight.
Our girls, good girls, have shaken off their trances.
They're over now forever, the long dances.
Only the moonlight, sober and real, advances
over our hills to touch my head with white.
They're over now forever, the long dances.
Our woods are quiet. The god is gone tonight.

Why We Drink

I tell Malik I'm going to stop. I tell him that I do it
because I am sad and because someone
was mean to me at a lecture after five men
spoke during the Q&A so I said something, finally,
about energy and petrocultures and didn't the infrastructure
of the moon landing look just like the oil fields
of Alberta and some older Italian man said no, said I was
projecting as if projection was not interpretation
but it was in front of a lot of people and what
was the point of all my degrees and giving up a decade
of life to school if I could be so easily humiliated and maybe
I shouldn't have worn jeans shredded at my thighs
or that navy sweater, sleeves blooming with moth holes
but if these are our left institutions, if these are the men
on our side, I said, then of course, I am going to drink.

Malik tells me you can't quit before thirty-five
because you're not going to stay quit
and something about me trusts him because
he was at the Far Inn back when it was the Ear Inn,
back in the old New York and he tells me I am
the new New York and I don't even know how
to tell him that I am not even that.
I say humiliation is like the nausea of childhood with
those delayed epiphanies. I hate the violence of insight—
how the lesson is always how one is ugly or dishonest,
the shortcomings that could build a civilization and then did.

Malik is not even so much older, forty-something but there have been
many Maliks and therefore he claims ancientness. He says it's all real.
My parents and those men and yes, even the feeble species.
He keeps a notebook and writes down all the great Irish bits
spiraling out of Helen's mouth at dinner. He sits cross-legged
on a pillow, cradles lemons and snacks on pickle, waxes poetic
while he assesses the spice level of a green Peruvian sauce I make
which he only ranks a three for spice but insists
that it is a ten in taste because he knows I am fragile.
He does impressions of nutritionists and people who get jazzed
about gym memberships but I know, though we are laughing,
that he is really sad. Sad that this is the theater of his multitasking,
that the corruptions are multiplying faster than our jokes
so we have become creatures who can slip through
dimensions, our times thick with simultaneity, so ready
we are to be brutalized many times a day. Even with laughter.
Malik says maybe it's time to leave New York. He can tell
we're all getting tilted there, and by that he means
becoming products, paralyzed by false moonlight in the streets.

I tell Malik I drink because I am tired and because they hate us anyways
and we are outside while others smoke at the opening
of the Red Wheelbarrow in Paris and I'm wearing a polka-dot dress
and I forgot to put on a bra this morning and it is freezing
and I see myself, the mess of my complaints and temperatures, the way
I am not making any sense these days. He says yes and yes and yes.
He keeps saying it is all okay, all real, tells me to turn my insights
into continents, into paintings. Get sloppy, delicate. Be a feral amateur.
When I get back to New York, he is the only one I still talk to on the regular.
He says *Listen to this* and *Read this* and his brain is so addicted to joy
and we both get nominated for a prize in the same week and it works
it really does work, the way his spirit skims octaves across the ocean
into my heart, into this poem, the way he said my Jesus year

now that I'm thirty-three is going to reveal something about me
which it just did and do you know, this time the revelation
didn't hurt so much. Which is what Malik might call aging
a process not nearly as dire as they want you to believe.

My Friend Says I Should Be Thinking About "Masked Intimacy" When I Think About Leila Olive

I am making an exception for the tree that fell in the storm. And the guy I hired to clean up the tree. And the limbs he left plunged deep in the yard. And the shape they make: a V.

Everyone agrees. Restaurant workers are *very exposed*.

On Tuesdays late, so 3 a.m., I sign into a Zoom where we sit around and read Lacan's *The Psychoses*. I am googling "what is masked intimacy?"

Cool your jets. Cool your jets. This is the phrase I most often think in regards to Leila Olive. And then. Cuddle with her. Something else with her. Ask her "Does this feel good? How about this?"

I don't really see the need to think about *masked intimacy* yet. Leila Olive works in a restaurant all the time and has a boyfriend and yeah, she's bi, and I've only seen her once. During the pandemic. In December.

First my ex was a watercolor above the fireplace. Then I moved her to the kitchen. I knew she'd hate that. But she'd like it better than being listed for sale on Etsy.

Having the hots for artists is a recurring problem for me.

When people say "recurring problem," do we actually mean "chronic desire"?

There's a squirrel on the V and he's eating a nut. I'm just reporting the facts.

This summer I had a weather phobia. No, worse than that. My partner—you can have more than one—had to look up the weather every day. If it was going to rain or storm, I got on the floor between sofa and coffee table and put a cushion over my head.

You could lie in the bathtub covered by sofa cushions, my therapist suggested.

It is very unlikely you will die from a tree crushing you during a storm.

All this medical in the pandemic is reminding you of your childhood. You did not have much choice.

But I know the truth: Zelda Fitzgerald went to a party. She was getting drunk and watching Scott flirt and she called the fire department. The party carried on. This was in the 1920s. She had been to several parties, was rich, from Montgomery, died right up the road from here in Asheville, North Carolina.

Finally, I got on buspirone and then I didn't care about the tree that I knew would fall and which did fall, but not on my house, and I didn't care about my lungs and I stopped taking the X-rays out of the closet to have a look at myself.

Are you practicing *masked intimacy*? Best I can figure you wear a mask and take off all your clothes. I don't take off all my clothes for anybody. It's not my thing. I like to have a long cape or tee shirt or latex thigh-highs still on me.

One person is not talking to me about *masked intimacy* at all: Leila Olive. The subject has not come up. Twice she said, *I'll get tested for you.* She said, *Send it to me. Send it to meeeeee.* She said, *I missed ya today at work.* And, *Ugh yr so hot I love you.* The next morning: *So embarrassing. I was drinking tequila.*

Hey. Cool your jets.

You're thinking I have Leila Olive on a pedestal and you're right. I can hardly go anywhere outside my brain. But this isn't Ancient Greece, so I do not imagine her cast in marble on a column in front of a temple.

More like on a blue velvet chaise lounge in a living room—not mine: there's a guy here, he's my partner; this is not for him—where she's wearing whatever she wants and bored by the poem she's reading.

When Auden said, "Every critic should state his Eden," he was basically saying, "Every poet should taste her Leila Olive."

She goes into work at 3 p.m. and gets off at 10 p.m. and sometimes makes $500 in tips.

I cannot actually imagine kissing Leila Olive through a mask. Okay, I have imagined it. If we must do it, we must. But I would like a pair of small copper-handled scissors nearby so we can cut the parts out of our masks for our lips. You're thinking, "That defeats the purpose."

But there's not a purpose here. This is not a business meeting.

So many red flags I could build a castle behind them.

Zelda's at the party and she's flirting too. She has forgotten about calling the fire department. She's talking about jazz to someone in that way white women have of wanting, so badly, to be conversant in Black aesthetic. The firemen arrive.

Nothing seems to be on fire. "Who called the fire department?" some guy shouts, relieved to finally have a thing to say at a party. "I did," Zelda says, and then that guy, for the rest of his miserable life, tells everyone he talked to Zelda Fitzgerald once at a party.

I did not know my own heart around Leila Olive in the before times. I thought she was standoffish, very smart, and of course I, and everyone in the room, recognized her beauty. I did not ever think of kissing her.

She does not champion her own beauty. Does it grieve her? Has she come to grief? Will she come to grief? Am I going to be involved here, somewhere, in this coming or this grieving?

Let's say you're right and I did think of kissing Leila Olive. It was so far back in my mind that it was like one of those Lacanian books. I would've had to look my index up to find the page of the kiss I imagined.

Index fingers are highly underrated. Trigger, slick, button, quick.

"I did," Zelda says. "Where's the fire?" this one fireman asks. And Zelda points to her heart. "It's here. It's right here," she says.

I don't know. I'd wear a mask and go to coffee with her. I'd wear a mask and go to her place. I'd wear a mask and watch a movie. I'd wear a mask and say, "Plz take off your mask" and she'd say, "We really shouldn't be doing this."

That's the phrase people use right before they really want to do something.

It wouldn't be sad without the ending. But you have to know the ending. For once, you get to know the ending. Zelda was in a waiting room. In Asheville, North Carolina. A waiting room for electroshock therapy. That's when the fire broke out.

Did she know, in advance, at the party, that there would be a fire and she would need those firemen?

Auden wrote privately to a friend, *Of course, I know Sappho's work has homosexual valences. But it's not time.*

On man-time, it matters who presides over the money and the weaponry. On crip-time, I send a GIF of two women kissing. She hearts it.

Sophie Klahr

After the War I Dreamt of Nothing But the War

When the nurse on the phone won't tell me
where you are, I turn my body into wind

   troubling the city of hospitals.
Slang of nurses, blood numbers, legalities;

my disease has made me fluent in Emergency;

at the front desks they are not allowed
to say you are here, but they do not say

you are not here, they say, *If he was here*
would you want to send back a note?

    and I write three notes
in three hospitals, watching the nurse

for her smooth head's small twitch that says,
    He isn't here.

It's Mercy Hospital, finally, that has you.
And again, because you are not family

I am a waiting room, crowded with sound.

Something-something-terror
jangles across the television: old news.

Two children, strangers, discuss superhero du jour:

Iron Man   Iron Man can   he can fly, he has guns, he can turn
into whatever he needs.

The crows have come back
to the city for the spring. They swerve

over each river, crying to one another

Come here come here come here come here
come here. Come here come here

Listening to the Radio, Driving Through Nevada Again

and thinking of how in the ocean once,
waist-deep, we fought. I had started drinking
again, trying to stop.   Was that the time
we stayed in a motel called The Sunrise?
White wicker, the peach-brushed walls, a prism
tied by fishing line to the fan so that
a jewel seemed to float mid-air? What year
was that   was that   the year he wrote *I can't
be what grounds you* ?   A song is slipping in—
   If you fall asleep down by the water—
Recall's accumulation swallows place.
(Or, tell it this way:) memory rips me
from the land. I miss an exit. I mis-
take this state for another. Take the wheel.

Drinking money

In 1939, when my mother was seven years old, the
lyricist Lorenz Hart gave her a photograph of himself on
which he had inscribed in midnight blue ink: *For Kathryn Jacqueline,*
from Lorenz Hart, whose name will probably be forgotten by the time she
is able to read this. Hart had been a friend of my grandfather's. My
grandfather, a
vaudevillian. I remember reading Hart's inscription for
the first time and thinking it was an extraordinary thing
for someone to say to a child—as if childhood had the
same kind of unpredictability and loneliness that fame
did. I inherited the photograph after my mother's death
and sold it to an autograph dealer on 18th Street for
drinking money. In the museum of saddest things I've
ever done, that could have been the saddest. It felt like I
was making fun of beauty.

Ghostwork

The body is everywhere.
He knew that when he let it go.
Suspend, the room said to the wire of mind
as it instructed the body.

I think I see him every day: just there: at the edge
of life: where it feels like work.

I think he comes forward through his death
anxious to mark a wall.

But I'm wrong. He wants to repeat a thing
so he can live beyond his taking—a habit, say—something
faulty, that won't catch light. There's Kevin, my twin brother,
one day sober, trying to light a cigarette in the wind.

The body is everything.

Sherwin Bitsui

The Caravan

The city's neon embers
stripe the asphalt's blank page
where this story pens itself nightly;
where ghosts weave their oily hair
into his belt of ice,
dress him in pleated shadows
and lay him fetal
on the icy concrete—
the afterbirth of sirens glistening over him.

We drain our headlights
on his scraped forehead
and watch the December moon
two-step across his waxen eyes;
his mouth's shallow pond—
      a reflecting pool
      where his sobs leak into my collar.

One more, just one more, he whispers,
as he thaws back into the shape of *nihitstilí*
bruised knees thorning against his chest.

We steal away,
our wheels moan
through sleet and ash.

Death places second, third,
and fourth behind us.

At home on the Reservation:
Father sifts dried cedar leaves
over glowing embers,
Mother, hovering
above cellphone light, awaits:
    He's okay,
      never went out,
      watched a movie instead.

But tonight,
my speech has knives
that quiver at the ellipses
of neon Budweiser signs
blinking through the fogged windshield,
and I text:
    I've only rescued a sliver of him,
    he's only twenty-five
    and he smells like blood and piss,
    his turquoise bracelet snatched for pawn,
    by the same ghost who traded his jacket
    for a robe of snow and ice,
    before inviting him
    back into the Caravan
      for *one more, just one more.*

Final Poem for My Father Misnamed in My Mouth

Sunlight still holds you and gives
your shapelessness to every room.
By noon, the kitchen catches your hands,
misshapen sun rays. The windows
have your eyes. Taken from me,
your body. I reorder my life with
absence. You are everywhere now
where once I could not find you
even in your own body. Death means
everything has become
possible. I've been told I have
your ways, your laughter haunts my mother
from my mouth. Everything
is possible. Fatherlight
washes over the kitchen floor.
I try to hold a bit of kindness
for the dead and make of memory
a sponge to wash your corpse.
Your name is not *addict* or *sir*.
This is not a dream; you died
and were buried three times. Once,
after my birth. Again, against
your hellos shedding into closing doors,
your face a mask I placed over my face.
The final time, you beneath my feet. Was I
buried with you then? I will not call
what you had left anything
other than *gone* and *sweet perhaps*. I am
not your junior, but I

survived. I fell in love with being
your son. Now what? Possibility
was a bird I once knew. It had one wing.

Where is the drug to drug this feeling out of me, the drug
to drug away the fear of drugs and what they steal from me
or stole from me, sometimes love and then my sanity, the frozen
bowling ball that set up shop inside my gut and liked it there
and never went away, I never went away for fear of losing
what I left which was itself a kind of hell, the hell of being
terrified of swapping hell for hell, my son, fucked up, rolled
his car in dark Ohio, lay inside the ditch and listened to the crickets,
even grass, he said to me, he could hear it growing, and corn, all
of it just trying to get by, as close as he could come, he said, to God,
and I was a such a fool, believing in fruition, stuck inside the fairy
tale of resurrection, even stars, he said, are trying to get by and then
he used for ten more years and bankruptcy and where's the melody
to remedy the melody, the remedy to remedy the remedy?

I aborted two daughters, how do I know they were girls,
a mother knows, at least one daughter, maybe one
daughter and a son, will it hurt, I asked the pre-abortion
lady and she said, her eyes were so level, I haven't been
stupid enough to need to find out, cruel but she was right,
I was and am stupid, please no politics, I've never gotten
over it, no I don't regret it, two girls with a stupid penniless
mother and a drug-addict father, I don't think so, I shot
a rabbit once for food, I am not pristine, I am not good,
I am in no way Jesus, I am in no way even the bad Mary
let alone the good, though I have held my living son
in the pietà pose, I didn't know at the time I was doing it
but now that I look back, he'd overdosed and nearly died,
my heart, he said, his lips blue, don't worry, I've paid.

Death Star

Angel of cocaine
Overdoses and middle-aged men
Discovered on floors, in bars,
In women's bathrooms—

Beneath a juvenilia of stars.

Quarantined Adderall and Michelob
Chasers.

If no one sees, does that mean
It never happened?

Getting off the medicine
Is like a religious experience,

But that doesn't make it religious, does it?

I hope you've collected all your lies
In your exquisite
Notebook.

Forming

Plastic baggy filled
With kiddy pills, I said
To Billy when I collect-called him
From the Exxon gas station.

Death's outrageous music is coming back into me.

When they came to the house and
Took away our father, they
Took his wallet with our pictures
And his Bic pens from his shirt pocket.

They put him in a bus and sent him
Into the flame of the desert.

Thirteen days with no food.
Nothing but Percocets and black
Martinis. Zombie drool wasteland, welcome

To the dream state
Called rescue.

There must be a room in this world—

Carità Americana

I found regret in a deli case;
it was white and shaped like a brick.
On the label a cow from Vermont
grazed on forget-me-nots or drank
from a pond. I can't remember which,
since it was the black splatters
—or was it white splotches—
I was taken with, and the thin legs,
and the elegant body shaped like a tank.
Although, what I remember most
is the missing udder, that pink fist
of gravity every Holstein swings,
whose absence could have been intended
because the artist hoped liberating his cows
from the bondage of breasts
(an act of charity, no doubt,
though not Roman; Hindu, maybe)
would impress the feminist he was dating
who was head over heels
for vegan babka.

The meat cutter offered me a taste,
because he saw how I kept staring
longingly in his case (as if I were starving)
at that blessèd cow without nipples
drawn by a lovesick artist in Jersey
who wanted me to believe it gave the milk
that made the immaculate cheese
now sitting in my hand,

whose taste I already knew well,
even though I played the naïf, even though
I knew better, that after I had chewed the last bite
of that sacred square, in two minutes' time,
maybe less, I would begin expanding,
but not with the Holy Ghost,
with lactose, in the small intestine,
so that by the time I reached my car
I'd be ready for the fiddle
because I would look like one of the demented
Roman emperors, the ones that were all paunch
and wild eyes and who had a taste for fire.

To the young meat-cutter waiting
for my answer, for five o'clock, for an escape
from the madness of fluorescent lighting,
I wanted to say *Thou*, wanted to be formal,
not because it rhymed with *cow*,
it was that magical beast after all that joined us,
but because we were beyond the quotidian now,
and biblical time is archaic
and thus it would only be proper to say, "*Thou*
slicer, *Thou* priest of the cold cut
who set me on the path
of suffering with an act of charity,
do you know your Vermeer, your Caravaggio
and Rubens, and thus the story
of Pero and Cimon, and how the one,
the grown child, fed the other,
her jailed father, in secret, with the milk
of her body, so that he wouldn't die
as had been decreed, from want, from lack
of food and drink,

and how when all was discovered
the father was released and the daughter's gift
was named *Carità Romana*?"

I mumble, "Thou, Thou," and then,
"No, thanks," because I'm already late
to visit my father in the hospital,
in his cold room which, in another country,
one thick with forests and secrets,
with caves to hide in from the authorities,
would be for enemies of the state.
He's a prisoner of his body
—his hunger is vulgar, beastly even,
but unlike Pero, there is no milk in my chest,
which I would let him cleave and suckle anyway
but for the bitterness swimming there.
He looks almost Roman now
with his buzzed head and marching veins.
For all his brio, he'll never teach another son
how to steal corn by moonlight,
just enough to eat and sell,
or how to build a house, or how to read
the soot marks on any brick
from the Great Chicago Fire of 1871.

When he wakes and adds his lowing
baritone to the shrieks and trills
of his neighbors down the hall,
I clear my throat and do my best cowbird
and watch his face cloud
with yearning, a naked shyness,
like the kind a calf wears
when it's startled by your voice

and it drops its mother's nipple to stare at you,
milk still hot on its tongue.
His sweet cow face is almost enough
for me to forget the old injuries,
how he laughed every time I retched
in the bathroom because of the butter
he hid in my food. No, I can't lie
and tell him what he wants to hear,
will not say that I love him, will not
admit to that. Instead, I'll wash his hair
and clip his nails, shave his face,
and when my traitorous lip trembles
with pity, I'll whistle
louder, longer, and teach him about regret,
feed it to him one note at a time,
and though he knows he shouldn't,
he'll devour it with the knowledge
that my song will swell and split his heart.

VI. Wisdom: The Voice of God

Ninety percent of what's wrong with you
    could be cured with a hot bath,
says God through the manhole covers,
    but you want magic, to win
the lottery you never bought a ticket for.
    (*Tenderly,* the monks chant,
embrace the suffering.) The voice never
    panders, offers no five-year plan,
no long-term solution, no edicts from a cloudy
    white beard hooked over ears.
It is small and fond and local. Don't look for
    your initials in the geese honking
overhead or to see through the glass even
    darkly. It says the most obvious shit,
i.e., Put down that gun, you need a sandwich.

Illiterate Progenitor

My father lived so far from the page,
    the only mail he got was marked OCCUPANT.
        The century had cored him with its war, and he paid
            bills in person, believed in flesh and the family plan.

In that house of bookish females, his glasses slid on
    for fishing lures and carburetor work,
        the obits, my report cards, the scores.
            He was otherwise undiluted by the written word.

At a card table, his tales could entrance a ring of guys
    till each Timex paused against each pulse,
        and they'd stare like schoolboys even as he wiped
            from the center the green bills anted up.

Come home. I'm lonely, he wrote in undulating script.
    I'd left to scale some library's marble steps like Everest
        till I was dead to the wordlessness
            he was mired in, which drink made permanent.

He took his smoke unfiltered, milk unskimmed.
    He liked his steaks marbled, fatback on mustard greens,
        onions eaten like apples, split turnips dipped
            into rock salt, hot pepper vinegar on black beans.

Eccles. 9:7

Go, eat your bread in gladness, and drink your wine in joy; for your action
was long ago approved by God.

In my favorite fantasy
I am given

permission   I am prone
face toward the light
beach queen   bathed in body

A thought that comes from a coming-from   the sweet place

where a sunset isn't indescribable
something simply looked at

The sun sets   I sit
sinless in sand
I sip only once

The Forty-Third Day

with lines from "Ocean of Earth" by Guillaume Apollinaire, translated by Ron Padgett

Today I got mad at a door

I did most of the talking

In the sunlight I sneezed

And reabsorbed the sneezes

I went to the room they suggested

Let's all look together

At our identical lonelinesses

Let's all ask new questions

How many holes do I have

How many corks are left

I like my whiskey messy

I kiss my wife without her diamonds on

I like a jug with a sturdy handle

The evening as it's turning brown

My bare ass bouncing to the bottom of the sea

I called my friend Dillon

I did not do most of the talking

I've begun to notice things

There's a rat in the trash room

Twelve minutes to twelve

Either my body is a bullet

That will not stop misfiring

Or I'm asleep in the crawlspace

Lapping at lead paint

I am the blood

And the surface to which

The blood is fixed

I am not the washcloth

I am not the soap

Lately fixated on

Two lines of Apollinaire:

I have built a house in the middle of the Ocean

Its windows are the rivers flowing from my eyes

I told Jerry today that sadness is the ocean

And depression is the wave

I was trying to be helpful

I think I'm two steps up the staircase (to where)

Can't be sure

Flatly I am refusing

To become my own gravedigger

Octopi are crawling all over where the words are

The commas mature into question marks

Who are you now without and

What do you think a girl really is

Amenorrhea or only "amen"

A man with a limp fist

A moon or a lamppost

A fleshy hourglass

Of wine glass of wine glass of wine glass of wine

A ceaseless white noise

Haunting rhythmic static

Maybe a girl is

Something that fucks up your sleep cycle

Something that smells like sweat

In the morning below a thin blanket

Something that sticks to the stubborn bone

I wore a silk blouse today

I wore lipstick I went to a museum

I woke up with a cup of tea

Good conversation with God in the afternoon

Conducted in

Bright but barely visible tufts of air traded back and forth

The plan is to give away

Everything I do not possess

And then see what happens

I went for a lazy walk

All the way to the other side of the island where

The beach is long and boring

I saw a kite in the sky but I

Could not see its master

Feet and sand and the strange warm

Light blue of low tide

Today

Once again

The legs that drove me into the room

Weren't mine

I was so grateful

I have a weakness for legs

One of my weaknesses

Dillon says I've arrived officially

But I don't know my zip code

For dinner

I threw lettuce into a bowl

And half a cucumber

Dried cranberries

Far too much dressing

I am bad at salad

But I am trying to get better

Legacy

And then there
are   those

who in the words of
a   r   t   i   s   t

Mendel-Black, "inherit
r e b e l l i o n . "

Large lots of unbeing-
p   a   s   s   e   d

down one generation to
the   next.

Absent value on the free
m   a   r   k   e   t

nothing gets resolved.

Too many other worries
a   n   y   h   o   w   :

the who what when
w   h   e   r   e

of basic living. Simple
names are expensive.

It   costs   too

much to be pronounced.
Best   yet

to curl under the weight

of obscurity, put on the
f   u   l   l

armor of mundane
Gods   who   see

fit to have their heirs
waste   away

among   brothers,
fattened from lamb

Ars Poetica, 1979

Digging in dregs of trash
to find the bird my father needed
to get well, I tore a vanishing
line across the length of my palm.
My hand emerged slowly,
crown of pulp, pulsing. My
excommunicated ex-Navy father:
Come here, Boy, (though I was a girl
he called me boy because
he wanted one). He pressed
his dirtied fingernail against
the head of the valley, dispensing
some trauma he'd picked up
in Vietnam about dead bodies
not being able to feel and pain
being the only true way to know

aliveness. How pleasure persuades
belief in a Heaven that doesn't
exist and how he could prove
God was fiction and Satan
the realest motherfucka ever
made: *Look around.* He lifted
his index, the one staunching
the flow, to his lip. Tasted my blood.
I let out something—more
moan than wail—too shaken
for much else when he grabbed
the back of my neck, pulled me

close to teach his only lesson
worth remembering: *Cry, Boy,*
look that honest wound in the eye
and you betta let this bitchuva
world see what she did to you.

A Controlled Substance

My brother is late again, somehow the glass
of water by his plate, the fact that we filled it
without him, makes him all the later. Dad
tells us to start eating, says there's nothing
worse than cold fish, but suddenly no one
can find a rhythm, we fumble our napkins
like we've never seen them before, like it's
just occurred to us we're in the wrong house,
aren't even a family but four people kicked
off the same bus for being vulgar. So much
is worse than cold fish, I think, the flowers
on the table, the bubbles in my brother's glass,
the size of our knives all terrible. "There must
be traffic," my mother says and I understand it
as a command. Yes, there must be. My brother
deserves a good reason. Not the only reason,
that he is deep in his bed, as if at the ocean floor
where it is still the first night on earth and
whatever moves there must grow its own light.

A Tour de Force

I got a book and can't
make myself read it, even
though my lover swears
it's good, even though
the cover says we might
all beautifully belong
somewhere. Imagine if
everything you saw was
printed inside your skull
where people could see it
after you died. When
you do a lot of cocaine
it feels like that's true, like
the gallery is struggling
to stay open because pipes
keep breaking and the floor
is always wet. That's what
I remember, anyway. It's
been a while since I had
enough money to be that
beautiful and echoing.
Of course, you can't find
anything in my head that looks
like a sunset or a toy horse,
it's all just goo in there,
that's what memories become,
dark water and milk. You
could no more read it back
than you could drink the ink
from a novel and know
who loved who.

Natalie Shapero

Good Share

An airport—like a hog farm,
like a landfill, like a graveyard—

has to go somewhere. An airport
has to go somewhere, so
why not here? I nominate you

and you and me to roil
in our respective beds while planes

fly so low overhead we can tell
what makes they are. The yowl
of the Airbus, the Boeing's

Gregorian roar. At least they drown
out the rest of this inexcusably human

night: longneck bottle greeting
the side of a passing car,
strange chanting, fistfight too close

to the tracks, the neighbors
with their nonstop innovation

in the arena of sex offender registry
drinking games. View the mug shot,
guess the offense, drink a shot if

you're wrong. Eleven men in ten
locations: guess which two guys

split a duplex. Drink a shot
if you're wrong. Plug in the ocean
in order to find out if anyone's

currently in the ocean and if
we, consequently, should avoid it.

Do you think we should avoid it?
Drink a shot if you're
wrong. Drink while you can,

because I heard from a dead guy
there's no alcohol in Heaven.

I also heard no alcohol
on Earth. If you're drinking right
now, buddy, you're in Hell.

Steven Espada Dawson

My Brother Stole Every Spoon in the House

so we don't eat soup anymore. We tried. The bone
broth fell right through our forks,

                our fingers, stained
the carpets. We all learned to speak twelve languages
but only the words for good morning

                    and hospital.
In Old Norse my mom learns the phrase where
are all the fucking spoons. Brian went outside, whispered
swears to the poplars.

            They bent their necks to hear him.
Brian went outside

           and left forever, took the rest
of the silverware. Brian went outside and left
a thousand doodles he drew,

             every happy animal
that wasn't him. We crumpled them like origami

           roadkill. Stomped them under our feet until
they became wine between our toes.
We're still drinking it now,

              ten years later. I don't know how
magnets work. If I tied a million together, could they
pull him here?

        The cutlery turned

              ash in his pockets.
That heavy metal in his blood.

At the Arcade I Paint Your Footprints

That summer we'd hop fences
and call them gates. You'd shark

pool, then we'd hunt deer
with all the quarters you tricked.

You smiled when they leapt
out of view. Passed me

that orange rifle, told me to aim
then close my eyes for ten years.

My antlered brother, mom
won't sell the house so you can

have a landmark. Nostalgia
rends in absence, and yet

I remember June—that last
game of foosball, how we broke off

the little men and shook them
in our hands like tambourines

hoping they'd wake, then run.

The Family Afterward

1. Cover Story

One pint is nothing
to a big man—
more than 200 pounds!
The liquor has to travel further,
dilutes, loses potency.
But what do I know?
Here's one thing—
Seagram's is a warm drunk.
Smirnoff or Absolut—cold.
He was smart enough to switch.
No more nastiness; he's
more himself, a gentle,
intelligent teacher
say all the student
evaluations.
You'd think *they'd* notice
if there was a problem.
Their comments are anonymous
and he's always
friendly to suggestions.
Once I asked him to open
a personal checking account,
leave the family funds alone.
NyQuil too, as in
Carver's famous poem.
It seems to have worked . . .
but I go to bed early,
what do I know?

Just this—he never once
touched the children,
laid a hand on my face
except with a kind of
removed tenderness.
Never smacked up the car,
except in his first
unhappy marriage. But then
he was unhappy.
We are not unhappy.
I am happy.

2. Toddler's Testimony

I wanted to hit him, but exactly I did not.

Ghosts were first. They all died. Then came dinosaurs. Then God
made people and I came out of Mom's stomach. I don't know where
Dad came from.

Yeah, my tongue keeps opening the door. He can't keep it shut.

Dad. Is he rich? I mean, he has all those teacups.

I was being chased by a tiger. Instead of running, I made a copy of
myself, filled it with a motor and sent it down the road. The tiger ran
after. I watched from a tree.

Through many dangers, toils, and snails, I have already come.

3. Shot Glass

Either way, he drank—
in defiance when I
refused him the cash,
square-hipped and loud
on swollen moral ground.
Or in gratitude
if I held my tongue
as he wobbled after
(no use counting)
another two-for-one.

Then, some vacation
the glass appeared—
in an upscale shop with
Depression-style dimples,
fairy-tale green.
I bought it for him,
but did not haggle;
the question no longer
was I accessory
but was I kind.

Overdose

All night I hold your driven body
Against some quantity of Quaalude.
A diner's red sign leaks in our window
To a wrist, to the essential curve of a stocking,
My twisted arms as I study your mouth
For breath. Trumped-up light lands
And flares as if to work significance
Into our profiles, in worrying down the night,
The ambulance not for us
While through your teeth a ruin of air
Begins its sad story to keep itself alive
And over and over the radio delivers
One message: forgive
And the rest will follow. My numb arms
Fold in with yours and myriad ways
Of how to wait this out
Stain the wall behind your head
As I guard this story, this tongue
I keep you from swallowing, thick with pulse,
The broken and insolvent music keeps
Round and round, halo of a headlight
Through trembling fingers. I have conceived
Of deeper alibis than even this.
I assemble to give myself
Nothing but the particulars with which
I will be finished.

From **WHEREAS**

WHEREAS I heard a noise I thought was a sneeze. At the breakfast table pushing eggs around my plate I wondered if he liked my cooking, thought about what to talk about. He pinched his fingers to the bridge of his nose, squeezed his eyes. He wiped. I often say he was a terrible drinker when I was a child I'm not afraid to say it because he's different now: sober, attentive, showered, eating. But in my childhood when things were different I rolled onto my side, my hands together as if to pray, locked between knees. When things were different I lay there for long hours, my face to the wall, blank. My eyes left me, my soldiers, my two scouts to the unseen. And because language is the immaterial I never could speak about the missing so perhaps I cried for the invisible, what I could not see, doubly. What is it to wish for the absence of nothing? There at the breakfast table as an adult, wondering what to talk about if he liked my cooking, pushing the invisible to the plate's edge I looked up to see he hadn't sneezed, he was crying. I'd never heard him cry, didn't recognize the symptoms. I turned to him when I heard him say *I'm sorry I wasn't there sorry for many things* / like that / curative voicing / an opened bundle / or medicine / or birthday wishing / my hand to his shoulder / *it's okay* I said *it's over now* I meant it / because of our faces blankly / because of a lifelong stare down / because of centuries in sorry;

Body of Magnesia

When the door between the worlds opened
I ceased to be a ghost, I became
the blood in my fingers in the veins of my hands
I felt the world under my feet
with its nails and its splinters I felt
The salt the red water in the loam of my chest I was

no longer a ghost, the vapors were gone,
I was solid, I hurt, my wings could be broken,
it was joy, I was living in it,
I bled, I cried.

Katie Jean Shinkle

Call Your Mother (*Fentanyl*)

This is where
    a *pop pop*
        is not innocent
            but the ring of the bell of death.
                Today
                  all the trees
                    have fallen off the leaves,
                      everything green,
gone.
        It's like that sometimes,
            where change is harder to hold,
                pressure enough
                  to stop my heart.
Hands to sky,
    a cry for help
        or celebration.

                      Close your eyes.

        God is a dope boy
        with a gun
        who doesn't know
        how to shoot it.

So hard
    to pin down.
      Keeping me   waiting.
          Offering   a high
             I have
              to keep chasing.

Blue Heart Baby

Everyone wanna put hands on a piece of your life.
Look at it: how it sags in the eigengrau,

like the yellow belly of a bitch heavy with litter.
No better than that meddlin-ass moon, full

as your own breast, hanging low between buildings.
People hang from the ropes your heart has let down.

The chaos of stars feels up the dead air. Tiny blue flames
in the eye bone of the young-old junkie girl

follow you around the floor of your humming days. &
have you seen yourself? *I think I am weak & without purpose,*

your father texts you from the kitchen, sauced up,
after he rolls his heavy body over the loaded pistol

he laid on your bed. *Get use to life.* Every piece
of advice is one the giver followed to his own

bitterness. You roll the heavy body of the car you loot
from your failed fiancé down the highway. Even

the wheel, wobbling with fury, insists on hanging on,
you must make it to each new mourning alive. Beyond

your silent mouth, what can you use to protect yourself?
The deceitful company of crowds will fail you, have you

out here with your young body, in the cold, a house
dress, barefoot on some other woman's back porch

where no one knows the address. Let it be,
if this moment is of use to your life. & how long

is a moment in time indistinguishable as speed—
peep the ant-sized airplane creeping across the crescent.

How to wake up the next day & the next & not simply
after a decade? After 13 blue moons? Stretched belly &

empty veins? The gas of constellations run out. Heart weighted
low in the sky. Your chances scattered across the dead years.

Redemption

after Charles Burnett's Killer of Sheep

Across the street, the Atlantic is draining from the harbor.
The aquatic pulse of the twelve million
going back. A voice washes into the bay—

It's my father. The father
I once lost, pulling me back from my single mind.
Dance with me, he is saying

at the bar beside me. Studying him,
I think about the Black worker: his grandfather,
a sharecropper in 'Bama, then a factory worker

at U.S. Steel in Cleveland, his father on the line
at White Motor Co., then later my father
first to think himself a citizen, signing up

to join the Navy, a specialist of machines.
I want to say the most important thing in the room
is the jukebox. But it is the sea, the tide starting to come back

into his eyes. *Dance with me*, he pleads
from that place we go to sip brown, slip the blue collar,
where four hours into the bottle he hears God's voice

and I hear his.   Now I'm 31 days sober deciding
to lead myself on this path beyond January. A Shepherd,
not a killer, or specialist of killing machines.

I study my father beside me at the bar
and I think of Stan in *Killer of Sheep*.
Stan back in Watts stringing up lambs

to feed his family and his daughter at home
dogfaced. Stan. My grandfathers. Time travelers
in the Great Migration, the peripatetic pulse

of the 6 million coming up. *Dance*
with your father, they are commanding me now
and I refuse with my eyes. I want to say

the most important thing in the room is the music,
but it is the water: Stan, chained to the small ship
of America's imagination, listing

on the restless sea of time. My father listing
drunk on the stool now, Blue Magic gas leak labor
coming out of his eyes, God

all around him, and the devil right with 'em, specters
tossing him back and forth—   until suddenly
(like that time in church, struck with glory

when he ran across the pews)
he is hopping up, stepping out onto the blue-lit
floor, yelling, *I'll dance alone! I'll dance*

alone! After all, I am an African.

Jeffrey Skinner

Fluctuations in the Field

I have only myself and the people in me. You know what I mean. I think I was one of the five hundred Jesus appeared to after he was raised, but can't remember my name or any details. Thomas in Aramaic, maybe. Before that, I went outside the cave and stared at the moon and clumps of stars while my woman and child were sleeping, praying under my breath Oh something something, give us alcohol so I can be taken away. Even then. For eons I'd pop in and out of existence, me and my dog Higgs Boson. Hey existence, I'd say, now I get it. And instantly an enormous child would appear and knock down my tower. The voice you're hearing as you read these words, for example, a voice no longer part of me—it's not part of you either. We are lost. We don't even know where the sound is coming from.

Reunion

Why do you keep returning,
alive, able to walk and gesture as you could not at the end,
your movements sketchy, more holographic
than warm? Thanksgiving dinner with all the relatives
and I alone with the suspicion I cannot speak:
You should be elsewhere.
Heavy drinking, as always. The newest baby
passed around like a contagious glow. Same teasing of the strong,
same muffled terror of the uncertain.
All the while you, at the head of the table like a signal
carried by a frayed wire—there, gone, there—raising a glass
to toast, the rim never touching your lips.

Anthony Ceballos

Until We Meet Again

Over there, my mother hides shaking body
on a shelf in a pried-open liquor cabinet.
And over there, my father climbs back into
the only Polaroid I have of him, buries himself
beneath a bunch of papers in a long gone
desk drawer donated to charity or trash.
And here, an only son seals himself inside
a bottle of water, wine, or Adderall,
throw me far from shore! he cries *far far away.*
And over there, my sister drives by in a beat-up
white car, she asks her boyfriend for a little more
money, prays to God for a little more time
and it's funny how she looks like our mom in the '90s.
And over there, my cousin dies when the car flips
over, somewhere only he knows, only sixteen,
only other cousin with two kids on the rez
tells herself tomorrow will be better, has to be.
Over here, I can't remember what they look like anymore.
And way up there, my grandmother makes frybread
for her boys, all in heaven, all gone too soon.
She saves a piece for grandpa on the other side
of the clouds, other side of town, way down below,
her number one grandson smells it through an open
window, tries to remember how a hug from her used to
feel, way back then, when things were simpler,
way over there, Saturday morning cartoons and a bowl of cereal.
And way up north, my uncle lies dead in a Duluth
hotel room, found by the woman he kept at his side,
they were homeless, broke and tired of running.

Back down here another uncle saves my ass with
a hundred dollars when he doesn't have to and I
let the words roll off my tongue, *nitroglycerin, please help,*
as in *not enough nitroglycerin he had a heart attack*
as in *uncle I'm poor need to get through the month please help.*
And in the mirror I see them all reflected
in a face I struggle to recognize, that person
over there stretches his mouth into a hideous laugh,
lunges toward my body to pull me through,
this ceremony of death while still alive, watch
the past burn to nothing and lament the childhood
apartment as it crumbles to dirt where so much
of my family lies in rest, and I come back to my senses,
pick up the glass, wonder what it's like to believe in God.

Listerine Dream

Peppermint please, or
give me spearmint, winter mint,
gum or candy mint
　　　as old lovers, ex-friends
clutch their arms
around me, forget
　　　my anger as we
　　　catch up, quick, meet
turn away as one straw
　　　snaps the camel's spine
and down goes your narrator, I
travel through fussy flowers,
night walks, there's
too much to forget, I have no ID,
no money but
　　　a treasure in the medicine
cabinet, poison control,
the storyteller asks
how do angels die? We can assume
in little rooms with locked doors
lights on and the drill of a vent,
with a twitching eye, a monotone death song,
I the speaker am the son
of drunk, cracked statue
glued together,
at the edge of shatter,
　　　of give up and choke
　　　on vomit the verge
　　　of anything or loss
　　　of everything

I ask does the sun exist
on the other side of cement?
                    We can assume no,
so smash the face into glass,
shove cardboard spoons down the throat,
weigh the body down with steel,
tell me no one cares,
                    at least my breath is fresh.

The Chute

When I was a kid, my father built a
hole down through the center of the house.
It started in the upstairs closet, a
black, square mouth like a well
with a lid on it, it plummeted down
behind the kitchen wall, and the raw
pine cloaca tip of it was
down in the basement where the twisted wicker
basket lay on the cement floor,
so when someone dropped in laundry at the top, it would
drop with the speed of sheer falling—in the
kitchen you'd hear that whisk of pure
descent behind the wall. And halfway
down there was an electric fixture for the
doorbell—that bell my father would ring and
ring years later when he stood at the door with that
blood on him, like a newborn's caul,
ringing ringing to enter. But back
then he was only halfway down, a
wad of sheets struck in the chute,
he could still fix the doorbell when it busted.
He'd stand his kids in front of him,
three skinny scared braggart kids,
and run his gaze over them, a
surgeon running his eyes over the tray,
and he'd select a kid, and take that kid by the
ankles and slowly feed that kid
down the chute. First you'd do a handstand on the
lip of it and then he'd lower you in,

the smell of pine and dirty laundry,
his grip on your ankles like the steel he sold,
he'd lower you until your whole body was in it
and you'd find the little wires, red and
blue, like a vein and a nerve, and you'd tape them together.
We thought it was such an honor to be chosen,
and like all honors it was mostly terror, not
only the blood in your head like a sac of
worms in wet soil, but how could you believe he would
not let go? He would joke about it,
standing there, holding his kid like a
bottle brush inside a bottle, or the
way they drown people, he'd lower us down as if
dipping us into the darkness before birth
and he'd pretend to let go—he loved to hear
passionate screaming in a narrow space—
how could you trust him? And then if you were
his, half him, your left hand maybe and your
left foot dipped in the gleaming
murky liquor of his nature, how could you
trust yourself? What would it feel like
to be on the side of life? How did the
good know they were good, could they look at their
hand and see, under the skin, the
greenish light? We hung there in the dark
and yet, you know, he never dropped us
or meant to, he only liked to say he would,
so although it's a story with some cruelty in it,
finally it's a story of love
and release, the way the father pulls you out of nothing
and stands there foolishly grinning.

Saturn

He lay on the couch night after night,
mouth open, the darkness of the room
filling his mouth, and no one knew
my father was eating his children. He seemed to
rest so quietly, vast body
inert on the sofa, big hand
fallen away from the glass.
What could be more passive than a man
passed out every night—and yet as he lay
on his back, snoring, our lives slowly
disappeared down the hole of his life.
My brother's arm went in up to the shoulder
and he bit it off, and sucked at the wound
as one sucks at the sockets of lobster. He took
my brother's head between his lips
and snapped it like a cherry off the stem. You would have seen
only a large, handsome man
heavily asleep, unconscious. And yet
somewhere in his head his soil-colored eyes
were open, the circles of the whites glittering
as he crunched the torso of his child between his jaws,
crushed the bones like the soft shells of crabs
and the delicacies of the genitals
rolled back along his tongue. In the nerves of his gums and
bowels he knew what he was doing and he could not
stop himself, like orgasm, his
boy's feet crackling like two raw fish
between his teeth. This is what he wanted,
to take that life into his mouth
and show what a man could do—show his son
what a man's life was.

Dana Roeser

Transparent Things, God-Sized Hole

All transparent things need
		thundershirts. The little
ghost hanging from an eave,
		on Underwood
Street, a piece of
		lavender-tinted
netting stretched onto
		a metal frame. The Boston
terriers and Chihuahuas patiently
		wait out storms
with their eyes bulging
		in their special
wraparound shirts. My
		family used to
laugh at me
		sleeping under
two down quilts, wearing a wool
		hat in summer,
when I said
		I was afraid
otherwise I would
		fly up to the ceiling.

Once on a sidewalk
		beside Erie Street
around the corner
		from Underwood
where the pointless
		obsolete

102

tracks run to a dead end
        on the other side,
I found a black
        and silver rosary,
with shining
        onyx beads, like
the ones
        that you see
hanging
        from the belts of
nuns in their habits or priests
        in their chasubles.
I kept it
        carefully until either
I lost it or it got buried
        in the bottom of a purse
abandoned under
        my bed or in the
closet. Clutter keeps
        me bound to this
earth.
        I told Patti last night
        that the God-sized
hole in me was
        so big and vacant,
voracious and spacious,
        it was like I was
running some kind
        of desperate toddler's
shape-sorter game, trying to find
        something that fit
to plug into it. I'd stuff anything
        in there, regardless

of whether the shape
        coincided with
the opening. It was
        like I could look
at the sky and attract
        space junk, broken
satellites, spent rocket
        stages,
micrometeoroids, to
        plug the
gap.

        The wind is its own
kind of chaos,
        sometimes like a sheet
of itself tangled
        or flowing
on a celestial
        clothesline. It needs
a weighted blanket.
        Little red flags
on the maple
        at the corner of
Underwood and Erie
        near the switching yard.
Slow-moving locomotives
        that might be driven by
nobody. Flags
        hold the tree down,
mark it, make it know
        it's real.
Flapping on the flaming maple
        or falling.

Track 1: Lush Life

The woman with the microphone sings to hurt you,
To see you shake your head. The mic may as well
Be a leather belt. You drive to the center of town
To be whipped by a woman's voice. You can't tell
The difference between a leather belt and a lover's
Tongue. A lover's tongue might call you *bitch*,
A term of endearment where you come from, a kind
Of compliment preceded by the word *sing*
In certain nightclubs. A lush little tongue
You have: you can yell, *Sing bitch*, and, *I love you*,
With a shot of Patrón at the end of each phrase
From the same barstool every Saturday night, but you can't
Remember your father's leather belt without shaking
Your head. That's what satisfies her, the woman
With the microphone. She does not mean to entertain
You, and neither do I. Speak to me in a lover's tongue—
Call me your bitch, and I'll sing the whole night long.

Erin Noehre

Tall, Pale, Wild Fall

I leave my room, go down the stairs and through the kitchen
of my childhood home,
where I live some days
with my Father.

I walk into the yard and find him
laboring something dead
shrubbed and yellow up and into
a gray industrial-sized garbage can

There is a new man inside him.
Living where the dark hit pulling
little levers and stops. Helping

my Father continue his small jobs
I look down to my hands. Glass-
wings afloat murder

My Father and I sit
in the front seat of my mother's car
He hands me a thin twenty
with instructions

Basic Full Flavor One Hundreds

A few blocks from here a girl is lying under-ground
still and clean   Above her a stretcher unbolts

and clicks
toward an open-wound.

Basic Full Flavor One Hundreds
I reach the money up to the counter.
Aren't you a little young for these?

the clerk says, his eye running over
my head

The day I was baptized my Father
carried me through Buffalo State Park

my eyes already
cane-black marbles of doubt

a mosquito globe swelling
between them.

Inside, on the mantle
my baby picture shows
a fading red blister

                                        "The jaws of life"
                                        are yellow

                                        You do not know this until
                                                you know this

I am sixteen, my Father is holding me in a hospital room
He is the first face who looks at me and knows
the boy is dead

Across from me now, he rests his hands.

I finally made it through
the birds the birds

December 21st 11:20:45 PM

I finally made it through the birds the
birds   the wings of rest   the *v* in the sky
the treads on treads   I finally made it
through the prisms I was trained to see at
3   the pictures of Lassie shaking in black
and white   the curtained haloes of purple
and red   the birds the birds   my guides
my sling out from the lakegray sky
leaving me to a priest of light   a port of
standing   the roads   the crest   the pier
the birds the birds   I know a reach   a
rule   a whisper   a liar   the trees   the
smoke   the two-story hopes   the
reservation of skies   the door to the
aviary where I finally made it through
where it took a farm   it took a chair   it
took all the took   a failure so great   all
the teeth   the tomorrows   the hands so
chapped and split from cleaning fluids   I
finally made it through the glass of scotch
the birds the birds flew off the pier   a
whisper over the water   it took a prism
and the first time I saw blue   I look back
as if this were the last time I will see these
rooms   the green glazes   the mustard
rugs   the tiny teacups and hanging glass

I made it through after having dropped
from the lakegray sky   I made it through
to the aviary where the birds flew away in
a whisper and I was left with a prism   a
draft in the eyes   I finally made it through
after I dropped from the sky by the side
of the road   our draft at a life   the
whisper   the halo   the tomorrows   the
birds the birds   the whisper of whales
of prairies   the moths   the windows   the
dirty walls

I have looked	something
about	
through prisms	great failures
I have seen	and great
freedoms	
the borders	so I would
know	
I have missed	the tryst
the train	the smile
if I don't know	the dead
lights	
the sky	the sky the
sky	
I will not	of so many
years	
know the sky	the trees
if I don't write	the smoke
the draft	our chapter
of our life	of hands

the draft   our prism
of tomorrows   of greens
will not come   my aviary
Mathias said   of birds

Standing at a Desk of Cranberries

Standing at a desk of cranberries   a small triumph of jumps   I wait longer than the rescue of rains   send prayers to the terror walking north

I do a pantomime on the edge of the cliff   reacting to the sea and the creatures in back of the house   if you had just looked out I would have said *this is my little resonance*

The guile of parrots   a carnival   a killing   a crusade   the final pursuit either a panorama or a demon

The fan click refuses to stop or to cancel its insistence   stubborn in the face of carnage   the fifty days of posters   all the field deaths   the once famous once child fortunes

Today not to beard but to wear black   today not to trace the creases on my face   today caught in parts   today to bicep toward justice   but not to beard as if that were even a possibility   even with lasers and goats   an ocean of black dogs and boats   searching for better swells   a more favorable forecast   a mast out of water   I want what the pelican sees

An answer comes in the smell of wood smoke as he passes by   a personal note at the slope of his neck   trials of bridges and the moon alongside Pont Marie I follow that smell with the O of sails and sorted shoes   with brushes and the corners of candles   a firm clap then the rubber stickiness of stones   I follow the tremble with the white noise of busses and a can of coins   surrounded by Joyce and daughter   blind on a broken chair   hearing cobbles

I'm just like you   some dying   some grief   some scotch   my final please unhooked from fire and earrings   knees in the grass   sinking into the sorted dirt   my beach a tree pleading with the summer surf   walking or chased   a finned orange fish that sucks at my sleep   a morning trail in lavender musk preacher mounds   a human fever   a corner room settled in blue plaid   a pot of red bowls   a curtain of frames   a pitted eye   a hill   a chimney   a pear

Where would these words be without a subject?   little carvings of mosquitos landing on my hands   headaches digging an elision of craters   a great empty blow of air that follows my feet   the big lumber of my dog's no longer here his hair an excursion that still flutters on the tile   slush and whispered breath where the naked man on the street washes his back with purple flowers

You keep saying *boy* like it's the belt that was used to tie you to the bed   you keep saying *bull* like you were forced to fight   you keep saying *dragon* as if courage had no sound   you keep saying *hair* and *crib* like babies come out of shells

A door to my back   the molding cheesy and rectal   I run with the horses across the field   the town wiped off the track and left behind   you curl up at the back of my neck and we go bucking over the whole knot of trails   the whole veiny land

The Great Blue Heron of Dunbar Road

That we might walk out into the woods
together, and afterwards make toast
in our sock feet, still damp from the fern's
wet grasp, the spiky needles stuck to our
legs, that's all I wanted, the dog in the mix,
jam sometimes, but not always. But somehow,
I've stopped praising you. How the valley
when you first see it—the small roads back
to your youth—is so painfully pretty at first,
then, after a month of black coffee, it's just
another place your bullish brain exists, bothered
by itself and how hurtful human life can be.
Isn't that how it is? You wake up some days
full of crow and shine, and then someone
has put engine coolant in the medicine
on another continent and not even crying
helps cure the idea of purposeful poison.
What kind of woman am I? What kind of man?
I'm thinking of the way my stepdad got sober,
how he never told us, just stopped drinking
and sat for a long time in the low folding chair
on the Bermuda grass reading and sometimes
soaking up the sun like he was the story's only
subject. When he drove me to school, we decided
it would be a good day if we saw the blue heron
in the algae-covered pond next to the road,
so that if we didn't see it, I'd be upset. Then,
he began to lie. To tell me he'd seen it when
he hadn't, or to suppose that it had just

taken off when we rounded the corner in
the gray car that somehow still ran, and I
would lie, too, for him. I'd say I saw it.
Heard the whoosh of wings over us.
That's the real truth. What we told each other
to help us through the day: the great blue heron
was there, even when the pond dried up,
or froze over; it was there because it had to be.
Just now, I felt like I wanted to be alone
for a long time, in a folding chair on the lawn
with all my private agonies, but then I saw you
and the way you're hunching over your work
like a puzzle, and I think even if I fail at everything,
I still want to point out the heron like I was taught,
still want to slow the car down to see the thing
that makes it all better, the invisible gift, what
we see when we stare long enough into nothing.

Reasons for Staying

October leaves coming down, as if called.

Morning fog through the wildrye beyond the train tracks.

A cigarette. A good sweater. On the sagging porch. While the family sleeps.

That I woke at all & the hawk up there thought nothing of its wings.

That I snuck onto the page while the guards were shitfaced on codeine.

That I read my books by the light of riotfire.

That my best words came farthest from myself & it's awesome.

That you can blow a man & your voice speaks through his voice.

Like Jonah through the whale.

Because a blade of brown rye, multiplied by thousands, makes a purple field.

Because this mess I made I made with love.

Because they came into my life, these ghosts, like something poured.

Because crying, believe it or not, did wonders.

Because my uncle never killed himself—but simply died, on purpose.

Because I made a promise.

That the McDonald's arch, glimpsed from the 2 a.m. rehab window off Chestnut, was enough.

That mercy is small but the earth is smaller.

Summer rain hitting Peter's bare shoulders.

The *ptptptptptptpt* of it.

Because I stopped apologizing into visibility.

Because this body is my last address.

Because right now, just before morning, when it's blood-blue & the terror incumbent.

Because the sound of bike spokes heading home at dawn was unbearable.

Because the hills keep burning in California.

Through red smoke, singing. Through the singing, a way out.

Because only music rhymes with music.

The words I've yet to use: timothy grass, jeffrey pine, celloing, cocksure, light-lusty, midnight-green, gentled, water-thin, lord (as verb), russet, pewter, lobotomy.

The night's worth of dust on his upper lip.

Barnjoy on the cusp of winter.

The broken piano under a bridge in Windsor that sounds like footsteps when you play it.

The Sharpied sign outside the foreclosed house: SEEKING CAT FRIEND. PLEASE KNOCK FOR KAYLA.

The train whistle heard through an opened window after a nightmare.

My mother, standing at the mirror, putting on blush before heading to chemo.

Sleeping in the back seat, leaving the town that broke me, whole.

Early snow falling from a clear, blushed sky.

As if called.

The Poets

Samuel Ace is a trans/genderqueer poet and the author, most recently, of *Our Weather Our Sea* (Black Radish) and *Meet Me There: Normal Sex and Home in three days. Don't wash.*, (Belladonna* Germinal Texts). A book-length essay, *I Want to Start by Saying*, is forthcoming from Cleveland State University Poetry Center (2024).

Chase Berggrun is a trans woman poet and educator and the author of *R E D* (Birds, LLC, 2018) and the chapbook *Somewhere a seagull* (After Hours Editions, 2023). Her poems and essays have appeared in *Poetry Magazine*, *American Poetry Review*, *The Nation*, and elsewhere. She lives in New York City alongside many houseplants.

Sherwin Bitsui (Diné) is the author of *Dissolve and Flood Song* (Copper Canyon Press) and *Shapeshift* (University of Arizona Press). He is of the Bįį'tóó'nii' Tódi'chii'nii clan and is born for the Tłizíłłani' clan. He is from White Cone, Arizona, on the Navajo Reservation. His honors include the 2011 Lannan Literary Fellowship, a Native Arts & Culture Foundation Fellowship for Literature, a PEN/Open Book Award, an American Book Award, and a Whiting Writers Award. Bitsui teaches for the MFA in Creative Writing Program at Northern Arizona University.

Sophie Cabot Black has three poetry collections from Graywolf Press, *The Misunderstanding of Nature*, *The Descent*, and most recently, *The Exchange*. Her next book is forthcoming in 2024. Her poetry has appeared in numerous magazines, including *The Atlantic Monthly*, *The New Republic*, *The New Yorker*, and *The Paris Review*.

Jericho Brown is the author of three books of poetry. His third collection, *The Tradition* (Copper Canyon, 2019), won the Pulitzer Prize for Poetry.

His poems have appeared in the *Nation*, the *Paris Review*, *Time*, and *The Best American Poetry*. He is the recipient of the Whiting Writers' Award, the National Endowment for the Arts, and the Guggenheim Foundation. Brown is an associate professor and the director of the Creative Writing program at Emory University in Atlanta.

Anthony Ceballos lives in Minneapolis and can be found penning staff recommendations at Birchbark Books & Native Arts. In 2016 he was selected to be a Loft Literary Center Mentor Series mentee. In 2022 he was part of the inaugural Indigenous Nations Poets retreat in Washington, DC. He is a first generation descendant of the Mille Lacs Band of Ojibwe.

Marianne Chan is the author of *All Heathens* (Sarabande Books, 2020), which was the winner of the 2021 GLCA New Writers Award in Poetry and the 2022 Association for Asian American Studies Book Award in Poetry. Her poems have appeared in *Poetry*, *New England Review*, *Kenyon Review*, and elsewhere.

Jos Charles is the author of *Safe Space* (Ahsahta Press, 2016), *feeld* (Milkweed Editions, 2018), a winner of the 2017 National Poetry Series and a Pulitzer-finalist, and *a Year & other poems* (Milkweed Editions, 2022). In 2016, Charles received the Ruth Lilly and Dorothy Sargent Rosenberg Poetry Fellowship from the Poetry Foundation. She resides with her cat in Long Beach, California.

Brendan Constantine's most recent collection is *Dementia, My Darling* (Red Hen Press, 2016). His work has appeared in *Poetry*, *The Nation*, and *Tin House*, among other journals. He currently teaches at the Windward School in Los Angeles and conducts workshops for writers living with Aphasia and traumatic brain injuries.

Cynthia Cruz is the author of seven collection of poems as well as *Disquieting: Essays on Silence*, a collection of critical essays exploring the concept of silence as a form of resistance and *The Melancholia of Class: A Manifesto for the Working Class*, an examination of Freudian melancholia and the working class. She lives in Berlin, Germany.

Steven Espada Dawson is from East Los Angeles. The son of a Mexican immigrant, he is the Halls Fellow in Poetry at the Wisconsin Institute for Creative Writing. Recipient of a Pushcart Prize and a Ruth Lilly Fellowship, his work appears in *Agni*, *Guernica*, *Kenyon Review*, *Ninth Letter*, and *Poetry*.

Megan Denton Ray is the author of *Mustard, Milk, and Gin* (Hub City Press, 2020), winner of the 2021 IPPY Awards Gold Medal and the 2019 New Southern Voices Poetry Prize. She holds an MFA from Purdue University. Her work has appeared in *Poetry*, *Adroit Journal*, *Passages North*, and elsewhere. She lives and teaches in North Carolina.

Martín Espada's new book of poems from Norton is called *Floaters*, winner of the 2021 National Book Award. He has received the Ruth Lilly Poetry Prize, the PEN/Revson Fellowship, and a Guggenheim Fellowship among others. A former tenant lawyer in Greater Boston, Espada is a professor of English at the University of Massachusetts-Amherst.

Megan Fernandes is a poet living in New York City. Her poems have been published in *The New Yorker*, *Ploughshares*, *The American Poetry Review*, *The Nation*, among many others. Her third book of poetry, *I Do Everything I'm Told*, is forthcoming in June 2023 with Tin House. She is an Associate Professor of English and the Writer-in-Residence at Lafayette College.

Sarah Gorham is the author of *Alpine Apprentice: A Memoir* (University of Georgia Press, 2017), which was a finalist for the 2018 PEN/

Diamonstein-Spielvogel Award for the Art of the Essay, and *Funeral Playlist* (forthcoming from Etruscan Press), as well as four collections of poetry. She is the recipient of fellowships from the National Endowment for the Arts, Yaddo, MacDowell, and others. Along with Jeffrey Skinner, Sarah is the co-founder of Sarabande Books.

Joy Harjo is the author of ten poetry collections and is an internationally renowned performer and writer of the Muscogee (Creek) Nation. She served three terms as the 23rd Poet Laureate of the United States from 2019-2022 and is winner of Yale's 2023 Bollingen Prize for American Poetry.

Mary Karr received poetry fellowships from the NEA, Radcliffe, and the Guggenheim. Her five collections include *Sinners Welcome & Tropic of Squalor*, the last long-listed for the Pulitzer. Her memoirs *Liars' Club*, *Cherry*, and *Lit* were *New York Times* bestsellers, as was *The Art of Memoir*. She's Peck Professor of Literature at Syracuse.

Sophie Klahr is the author of *Two Open Doors in a Field* (Backwaters Press) and *Meet Me Here at Dawn* (YesYes Books). She is the co-author alongside Corey Zeller of *There is Only One Ghost in the World* (Fiction Collective 2), which won the 2022 Ronald Sukenick Innovative Fiction Prize. She lives in Los Angeles.

Michael Klein's latest book *The Early Minutes of Without: Poems Selected & New* will be published in 2023. He lives in Rhode Island, currently curating a reading series with Spencer Reece and ghost writing a book of true crime.

Dana Levin is the author of five books of poetry, including *Now Do You Know Where You Are* (Copper Canyon Press), a 2022 *New York Times* Notable Book. She serves as Distinguished Writer in Residence at Maryville University in Saint Louis.

Ada Limón is the author of six books of poetry, including *The Carrying*, which won the National Book Critics Circle Award for Poetry. Limón was also the host of the critically-acclaimed poetry podcast, *The Slowdown*. Her new book of poetry, *The Hurting Kind*, is out now from Milkweed Editions. She is the 24th Poet Laureate of The United States.

Zach Linge is a visiting professor at Meredith College and the recipient of scholarships to the Kenyon and Sewanee writer's workshops. Linge's poems appear in *The Atlantic*, *Ploughshares*, and *Poetry*. Before teaching college English, Linge wrote daily news-analysis briefings for President Biden, Vice President Harris, and senior White House personnel.

Layli Long Soldier is the author of *Chromosomory* (Q Avenue Press, 2010) and *WHEREAS* (Graywolf Press, 2017). Her poems have appeared in *POETRY Magazine*, *The New York Times*, *BOMB*, and elsewhere. She is the recipient of the 2018 PEN/Jean Stein Award, the 2018 National Book Critics Circle Award, an NACF National Artist Fellowship, a Lannan Literary Fellowship, and a Whiting Award, among others.

Airea Dee Matthews is the author of *Bread and Circus* (Scribner Books, 2023) and *Simulacra* (Yale University Press, 2017), selected by Carl Phillips as the winner of the 2016 Yale Series of Younger Poets. Matthews is a Cave Canem Fellow and a Kresge Literary Arts Fellow, as well as the recipient of the Rona Jaffe Foundation Writers' Award, a Pew Fellowship, and the 2017 Margaret Walker For My People award.

Joshua Mehigan's second book, *Accepting the Disaster*, was cited in the TLS and *New York Times Book Review* as a best book of 2015. He has received fellowships from the NEA and the Guggenheim Foundation. From 2017 to 2020 he taught poetry at Northwestern University. He lives in Brooklyn, NY.

Tomás Q. Morín is the author most recently of *Machete* and *Let Me Count the Ways*. He has received fellowships from the Guggenheim Foundation and the National Endowment for the Arts. He teaches at Rice University.

Erin Noehre holds an MFA in Creative Writing from Arizona State University. She has received fellowships from the Center for Imagination in the Borderlands as well as the Virginia G. Piper Center for Creative Writing. In 2020-2021 she was a June Jordan Teaching Fellow at ASU. Her work has been featured in *Pidgeonholes*, *Sonora Review*, and *Passages North*.

Sharon Olds is the author of thirteen books of poetry, most recently *Balladz* (2022), a finalist for the National Book Award, *Arias* (2019), short-listed for the 2020 Griffin Poetry Prize, *Odes* (2016), and *Stag's Leap* (2012), winner of the Pulitzer Prize and England's T. S. Eliot Prize. Olds teaches in the Graduate Creative Writing Program at New York University. She lives in New York City.

Joy Priest is the author of *Horsepower* (Pitt Poetry Series, 2020), which won the Donald Hall Prize for Poetry. Priest has received a National Endowment for the Arts fellowship, a Fine Arts Work Center fellowship, and the Stanley Kunitz Memorial Prize from the American Poetry Review. Her poems have appeared in the *Atlantic*, the *Nation*, and the *Kenyon Review*, among others. She is the editor of *Once a City Said: A Louisville Poets Anthology* (Sarabande Books, 2023).

Dana Roeser's fourth book, *All Transparent Things Need Thundershirts*, won the Wilder Prize at Two Sylvias Press (2019). She has received the Great Lakes Colleges Association New Writers Award, the Jenny McKean Moore Writer-in-Washington Fellowship, and a National Endowment for the Arts Fellowship, among others. She teaches in the MFA program in poetry at Butler University. Poems have appeared in *Poetry*, *Crazyhorse*, *Denver Quarterly*, and elsewhere.

sam sax the author of the forthcoming books: *PIG* (2023, Scribner) and *Yr Dead* (2024, McSweeney's), as well as *Madness*, and *Bury It*. They live in Oakland with their sweetheart and giant dog and currently serve as a Lecturer at Stanford University.

Diane Seuss's most recent collection of poems is *frank: sonnets* (Graywolf Press 2021), recipient of the Pulitzer Prize. Her sixth collection, *Modern Poetry*, is forthcoming from Graywolf Press in 2024. Seuss was raised by a single mother in rural Michigan, which she continues to call home.

Natalie Shapero is the author, most recently, of the poetry collection *Popular Longing*, and her writing has appeared in *The New Yorker*, *The New York Review of Books*, *The Paris Review*, and elsewhere. She lives in Los Angeles.

Katie Jean Shinkle is author of five books, most recently *Tannery Bay* (with Steven Dunn, FC2/University of Alabama Press, forthcoming). She teaches in the MFA in Creative Writing, Editing, and Publishing program at Sam Houston State University.

Jeffrey Skinner's most recent book of poems is *Chance Divine*. A Guggenheim Fellow, and recipient of an American Academy of Arts & Letters Award for literature, his poems have appeared in *The New Yorker*, *The Atlantic*, and *The Paris Review*. Along with Sarah Gorham, he is co-founder of Sarabande Books.

From New Orleans, **Bernardo Wade** currently serves as editor and creative nonfiction editor of *Indiana Review*. Recently awarded the 2021 Puerto del Sol Poetry Prize, he has words in or forthcoming in *The Nation*, *Crazyhorse*, *Black Warrior Review*, *Guernica*, *Cincinnati Review*, *Southern Review*, *Ecotone*, and elsewhere.

Afaa M. Weaver (尉雅風) was born in 1951 in Baltimore, Maryland. His many publications include *Multitudes* and *These Hands I Know*, both from Sarabande Books. Afaa's newest work is *A Fire in the Hills* (Red Hen) his sixteenth collection of poetry, preceded by *Spirit Boxing* (U Pitt). He lives in upstate New York with his wife, Kristen Skedgell Weaver.

The Cyborg Jillian Weise is the author of *The Amputee's Guide to Sex*, *The Colony*, *The Book of Goodbyes*, *Cyborg Detective*, and *Give It to Alfie Tonight*. Cy directed the film *A Kim Deal Party* which screened at Public Space One. She will go by Cy, as a name, until disabled people are recognized as the first cyborgs all the way back to Hephaestus.

Phillip B Williams is a Chicago, IL native and author of *Mutiny* (Penguin, 2021), winner of the American Book Award, and *Thief in the Interior* (Alice James Books, 2016), winner of the 2017 Kate Tufts Discovery Award and a 2017 Lambda Literary award. He received a 2017 Whiting Award and was a Helen Putman fellow for the Radcliffe Institute for Advanced Study. He is founding faculty of Randolph College low res MFA.

Ocean Vuong is the author of the poetry collections *Time Is a Mother* (Penguin Random House 2022) and *Night Sky With Exit Wounds* (Copper Canyon Press 2016), the winner of the 2017 T.S. Eliot Prize. His novel, *On Earth We're Briefly Gorgeous* (Penguin Press 2019), was shortlisted for the 2019 Center for Fiction First Novel Prize and won the 2019 New England Book Award for Fiction. He received a Whiting Award in 2016 and a MacArthur fellowship in 2019. He is on faculty in the MFA program at the University of Massachusetts, Amherst.

The Editors

photo by Hien Minh Nguyen

Kaveh Akbar's poems appear in *The New Yorker, The New York Times, Paris Review, Best American Poetry,* and elsewhere. He is the author of two poetry collections: *Pilgrim Bell* (Graywolf 2021) and *Calling a Wolf a Wolf* (Alice James 2017), in addition to a chapbook, *Portrait of the Alcoholic* (Sibling Rivalry 2016). He is also the editor of *The Penguin Book of Spiritual Verse: 100 Poets on the Divine* (Penguin Classics 2022). In 2024, Knopf will publish *Martyr!*, Kaveh's first novel. In 2020 Kaveh was named Poetry Editor of *The Nation*. The recipient of honors including multiple Pushcart Prizes, a Civitella Ranieri Foundation Fellowship, and the Levis Reading Prize, Kaveh was born in Tehran, Iran, and teaches at the University of Iowa and in the low-residency MFA programs at Randolph College and Warren Wilson.

Paige Lewis is the author of the poetry collection *Space Struck* (Sarabande 2019), cited as "One of the best debuts of the year" in "Must-Read Poetry, 2019" by *The Millions*. They are a recipient of the 2016 Editor's Award in Poetry from *The Florida Review* as well as a Gregory Djanikian Scholarship from *The Adroit Journal*. Their poems have appeared in *Poetry, American Poetry Review, Ploughshares, The Georgia Review, Best New Poets 2017,* and elsewhere. They currently live and teach in Iowa City, IA.

Sarabande Books is an award-winning nonprofit independent literary press headquartered in Louisville, Kentucky. Established in 1994 to champion poetry, fiction, and essay, we are committed to creating lasting editions that honor exceptional writing. With over two hundred titles in print, we have earned a dedicated readership and a national reputation as a publisher of diverse forms and innovative voices.